# CHANGES

Written by **Marjorie N. Allen** and **Shelley Rotner**

Photographs by **Shelley Rotner**

**Macmillan/McGraw-Hill School Publishing Company**

New York Chicago Columbus

**Macmillan Publishing Company**
866 Third Avenue,
New York, NY  10022

**Collier Macmillan Canada, Inc.**
1200 Eglinton Avenue East, Suite 200,
Don Mills, Ontario M3C 3N1

For information regarding permission, write to
**Macmillan Publishing Company,**
866 Third Avenue,
New York, NY  10022.
This edition is reprinted by arrangement with **Macmillan Publishing Company.**

The text of this book is set in 20 point Jensen.
The photographs were taken on 35mm Kodachrome film and reproduced
from color transparencies.

**Macmillan/McGraw-Hill School Division**
10 Union Square East
New York, New York  10003

Printed and bound in Mexico.
ISBN 0-02-274905-5
6 7 8 9 REY 99 98 97 96 95

For Dena with love
—M.N.A.

For Emily and Stephen,
the best changes in my life
—S.R.

All things go through changes

as they grow.

From fiddleheads to uncurled ferns,

scattered pinecones — forest tall;

flowers peek through one last snow

as winter's gray turns to green.

Milkweed clusters bloom in spring;

and feathered seeds in autumn
dance lightly in the wind.

Sun gives way to clouds,
clouds and wind to rain,

and winter's cold brings
ice and snow.

Seasons change —

leaves fall.

Spring blossoms yield summer fruit;

in autumn, corn grows high.

All things change,

then change again.

From fragile eggs

to birds

in flight,

from spotted fawn to great-horned buck,

and piglet small

to giant sow.

Horses, too — foal to mare.

All things

go through changes

as they grow.

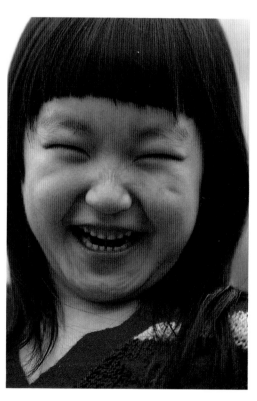